VACATIONS for the SOUL

Opening Doors to Places You Didn't Know Existed

by
MAX KARIMBEIK

www.maxtravelclub.com

All rights reserved. No part of this book may be reproduced in any form, by Photostat, microfilm, xerography, or any other means, or incorporated into any information retrieval system, electronic or mechanical, without the written permission of the copyright owner.

Disclaimer: The website www.maxtravelclub.com is the only contact given for travel because the nature of such information, address, phone numbers, dates, and other details are liable to change. The website is the best way to stay updated.

Copyright © 2012 Max Karimbeik

All rights reserved.

ISBN: 0615622127
ISBN 13: 9780615622125

Dedicated to my father, who believed in my vision first—thanks, Dad, for making it happen; my sweet and loving mother; my brother, whom I prayed for before he was born because when I was young, I always wanted a brother I could play with. Gabriel Kahsay, my soul brother and best friend— if it wasn't for you I wouldn't have been mentally ready to write this book. **Billy Monroe**, *the art master, for turning my vision of a raccoon into a reality: such a talented artist you are. I'm lucky to have found Billy Monroe and seen his talent before Antonio Villaraigosa, the mayor of Los Angeles, prized him for his work.*

Contents

1	The Journey Begins	1
2	Benefits of Max Travel Club vs. Flying Solo	9
3	Max Travel Club: A Mutual Admiration Travel Society, that's Opening Doors to Places You Didn't Know Existed	17
4	Holistic Travel	23
5	Spiritual Vacations for the Soul	31
6	The World Is Ours: Vacations to Give Back	43
7	Health Is Wealth and Healing Vacations for the Soul	45
8	Vacations That Heal the Soul	49
9	Health-Promoting Vacations	57
10	My Body Is the Temple of My Soul	63
11	Self-Improvement Vacations	71
12	Thousands Now Enhance Their Relationship Who Never Thought They Could	81

CHAPTER 1

The Journey Begins

"Traveling brings you closer to reality and to the world and connects you with your source. Why? Because people who travel to new places are usually in the present moment, not the past or the future. Traveling is like meditation."

—MAX KARIMBEIK

"Assume the feeling of your dream before fulfilled! And if you're so far away from that belief that you don't believe it, keep being 'persistent' with it until you believe it."

—DR. WAYNE DYER

In order for your mind, body, and spirit, which are interconnected, to be in balance, you need to feel like you're growing in all five areas of your life: spiritually, emotionally, physically, in your relationships, and financially.

All the life-changing vacations described in this book are important, because if you don't live from a high level from one area of your life, you can't live at a high level from another area of your life, at least not for long.

For those looking to get more from their lives and their vacations, consider that there are a number of active adventures—spiritual retreats as well as workshops—out there waiting for you to discover.

With that in mind, think about what you did for your last vacation. Can you even remember it? Many people will find that their last vacation consisted of nothing more than a tan that faded after a couple of days. The relaxation and peace you found while vacationing disappeared in just a couple of weeks. Soon you were doing your daily routine and were left merely with some random memories and souvenirs that don't have a lasting or direct impact on your life. For a while the pictures and shirts may help you remember the way you felt at that moment in your life, but they are just a reminder of a time you once had, and soon, like all the souvenirs you got in the past, they collect dust until they are so far in the past that you move on.

But there is a way for you to achieve permanent and meaningful changes in your life through travel. When you join Max Travel Club and study this book, you will discover new ways to improve your life—new skills and perspectives to take with you even when your vacation is over. The type of travel I will describe goes beyond simple time in the sun and seeing the sights. Instead I will focus on a total-body experience that delivers maximum results, and all with the Max Travel Club concept that will allow you to discover new things that help you grow, learn, and heal as well.

A vacation is a time to discern the reason for your life. It is not running away from hard issues but rather taking time to face those issues. Having more distractions and things to do make this discernment much harder, unless we seek vacations that open our lives to deeper dimensions. A real vacation should naturally address the big questions in your life without forcing you to think about them. The answers to these questions should just come to you: Does my life matter? What am I here for? Am I making the right decisions? What do I really value? Is God real? And so on.

Taking time to deal with yourself is more important than any other activity you're dealing with in your life right now. How can you possibly give to others and the rest of the world when you haven't given to yourself? All your demanding responsibilities can be handled so much better when your life is focused. I got to know a very successful man who had a remarkable ability to work eighteen hours a day and still look so alive and abundantly powerful. He told me he regularly went away on a vacation for his soul.

Your religion or faith should have nothing to do with joining Max Travel Club and taking a vacation for your soul. Your own personal faith can sometimes grow best when you leave behind the crowding demands of over commitment. If you truly love yourself, you need to keep daily life from smothering your soul. One of my favorite philosophers, George Santayana, said, "Society is like the air, necessary to breathe but insufficient to live on."

It is a given that your current vacation practices are going to be easy to continue. In fact, you might keep going to the place year after year. Maybe there's a spot at the beach you can't get enough of, or the mountains hold some wonder and mystery for you. You might just need to pick up the phone and call the same travel agent to take care of business. But the process can be just as simple when you join MaxTravelClub.com. In fact, you will find it is different from any other club you've seen in the past. The skills and knowledge you acquire on these travels, and the insights or talents you discover, will continue to impact your life. Even if you do nothing, these powerful destinations will influence you by themselves.

Let's take a moment and reflect on a quote that remains one of my favorites. It is by Earl Nightingale: "If you want to do what's right in order to be successful, you have to look at what the majority of people are doing, and do the exact opposite." I find this remains true for vacations and anything else in life. Most people aren't content with what their vacation offers in a week or two. Therefore, it is necessary to get the most out of whatever time offers you.

Let's assume you didn't have access to this book. You would have to put in extra effort to find such a vacation experience. A number of the vacations listed on MaxTravelClub.com won't be found through a travel agent. They don't appear in the pages of a magazine, and you will have a tough time finding advertisements for many of the retreats as well. In fact, there is a good chance your friends and family have no idea any of this exists, either. These vacations are best-kept secrets that only about 1% of the population have discovered.

Of course, there is a very good chance that you are going to end up going beyond your traditional comfort zone. You may try to stick with what you know and avoid taking chances. It can be a very relaxed and stress-free way to keep with your routine. Even when you have access to the various vacation destinations as a member of Max Travel Club, you may not have a full understanding of what to expect. When you dive in and begin to participate, however, you begin to have a remarkable experience enhanced by this hands-on involvement. Or you can be completely hands-off and still experience the power of being touched at a spa. Health counselors, even religious leaders, now promote bodywork to promote renewal and healing.

Harvard professor Dr. Deepak Chopra once explained that the purpose of life should be the expansion of happiness, and to remain in a state of happiness, you need to keep stepping into the unknown. The traps we face come from what we already know. Because we trust these things and know that we are going to enjoy them, we fear taking the steps towards change. But if we can work past that and try a new journey, like those offered through Max Travel Club, we can begin to touch these unknown areas and add a level of depth to our lives as we connect with new people who might share similar experiences to our own.

* * *

So the question becomes, are you ready to take that step into the unknown?

There is no doubt that you will be challenged in new ways during this process, and these vacations aren't going to be among the standard ones you are used to. Instead of meandering through a museum, you might take a more active approach, learning about your self-reliance and your confidence as well. Discovering ourselves is the greatest adventure of our lives, and to begin this journey we need to discover what adventure really means. This might be done through whitewater rafting, kayaking, rock climbing, or hiking in the Himalayas; swimming in the wild ocean; sleeping alone (or with our travel club) in the desert; passing through the Andean or dense Amazonian jungle. Luxury accommodations and first-class cruises with activities will give you lots of time for reflection and meditation while staring at the starry night, connecting with life from other parts of the universe. Like Albert Einstein said, "The most beautiful thing we can experience is the mysterious." A good travel society opens doors to other worlds for your soul. You're welcome!

Another choice you will have is to be like Henry David Thoreau, trekking "to the woods because I wished to live deliberately, to front only the essential facts of life, and see if I could not learn what it had to teach." Which basically means you can head through the forests of a National Park learning survival instead of remembering to slap on some sunscreen on the beach. Or, if you don't want to change your plans of hitting the ocean, you can take part in a swim with the dolphins to enhance your level of creativity as well as communication.

When you look at your past vacations, think about how deep in it you had to go mentally. I'll bet the hardest thing you thought about was remembering which SPF to buy, or which restaurant you were going to eat at that night. But if you want to add new skills to your life, skills you can take as useful mementos into the future, you have to move forward. In so doing, you will see the world a little differently, and the world will be a little different because of you.

Perhaps your last vacation offered you a very minor level of interaction. You may have spent time with family and friends, but never went past the comfort of your intimate group. But with these spiritual vacations, you can go beyond that. In fact, you will be able to connect with people on a new level (as long as you aren't going on a meditation trip to the desert, that is). You will meet new people and make new friends, people with the same mind frame as you have. Just keep in mind that not every vacation choice will be right for every member of your family. Some will encourage you to bring your spouse, your kids, and/or your parents.

Don't let the various items in this book scare you away. Instead, be sure you invest time and effort in the process. This can be social, intellectual, spiritual, emotional, or even physical. Each kind of effort will offer a unique return to you as you learn about the different vacations that interest you. Be sure to look for programs that meet your needs, the ones that will maximize the experiences you can take back into your usual life.

Don't be nervous about these experiences; they are designed to be enjoyable. There is little doubt that they will entail the same fun and relaxation of your standard vacation. Even though there are rigorous programs in this process if you choose, you will find that they still have recreation. A great number of the retreat areas, adventures, and centers are in scenic locations near oceans, mountains, lakes, and even farms. You will make new friends and have plenty of good food to share.

Max Travel Club will lead you to a vacation that will become a positive change in your life. You might unearth a new skill or hobby, and improve your health or spirituality to boot. You will embark on a vacation you will never forget, because you will enter a new world.

CHAPTER 2

BENEFITS OF MAX TRAVEL CLUB VS. FLYING SOLO

In the travel industry people who have vacationed in groups have proven higher satisfaction rates, which makes us happier clients. One reason is because we have similarities in our style of travel, and share a common interest together.

Members of Max Travel Club will receive amenities such as extra products services and benefits that individuals/couples and regular passengers/guests don't receive when traveling by themselves. We will also receive multiple forms of transportation included in one trip that you won't receive for free if you're a regular passenger not a part of our travel club.

1. Great Reasons for Joining Max Travel Club
2. It's just a great value, with all the added benefits and amenities!
3. You can socialize with your new friends or bring your own.
4. You meet new people with common interests, so you feel safer.
5. You are helping a cause.

6. You will consistently experience new activities unique to the group.
7. You will enjoy all the regular benefits of a vacation

My personal top two favorite amenities for the group are a cocktail party and wine at the table. Most businessmen think, act, and react like this life is everything, while most mystics completely detach themselves from this physical world as if it were nothing. Both extremes are wrong, because there needs to be a balance in every area of our lives. To put this in perspective, sometimes you feel like you need to socialize, and sometimes you feel like you need silence and your own space.

Anthony Robbins said, "People's standards are a direct reflection of the expectations of their peer group." So I say, love your family and choose your peer group. This is exactly why Max Travel Club was created. Traveling brings people closer together, and what better way to bring quality into your circle, with people who are living life at the highest level?

Scientific studies show that if you count your five closest friends five years from now, you'll be making as much money as your friends. This basically means choose friends that have higher standards than you in all areas of their life whether it's through Max Travel Club or on your own. Since we live in the west, we receive many examples that deal with money, but the same principles that apply to money can be applied to every other area of your life. Let's face it, if you're not balanced in all the areas of your life, your finances will also suffer. One main reason is because you lose your passion and drive to attract abundance into your life in the first place. There definitely needs to be a balance.

In order to be successful and content, you have to continually expand spiritually, emotionally, mentally, physically, and of course financially. What better way than to actually be a part of a club that supports your growth because its members are on the same page as you?

"Tell me who your friends are and I'll tell you who you are and what your identity is." So said Saidi, who traveled the world 800 years ago. An admirer of Aristotle, Saidi was wise enough for the king of Persia to ask him to be the prime minister of his empire. Saidi's words are something I think about because I choose my friends carefully and only associate with very few individuals. Obviously I invite anyone to consider my travel club, and if you're reading this book, you're clearly a bright individual interested in expanding yourself. If you stick with the club you will have potential to grow beyond belief and eventually be considered brilliant. A bold claim, yes, but if you consistently improve in every area of your life, it only makes sense that you will reach brilliance. Repetition is the mother of skill; time and patience are necessary for effective change. For change to last, traveling for the same purpose five times or more every year is quite sensible.

※ ※ ※

The benefits of an enlightening and renewing vacation are available to everyone. There were certain things I did personally to enjoy the benefits of a vacation even when I couldn't go anywhere. I myself didn't have an unlimited travel budget or spare time because of financial challenges, family, work commitments, and health issues due to chest pains from stress and literally not being able to move my body for a while because of a lower back injury. You don't need to buy a $2,000 plane ticket. A vacation for the soul is about movement, like a walk in the park.

Nature was my best therapy. Starting a relationship with a tree, going to the ocean, park, mountain, or lake helped me balance my mind, body, and spirit. In natural settings, answers to questions would come to me without my even trying. Nature was the best place for me to see how I'd matured, evolved, and changed. It's not exactly what you do or where you go as much as it is the attention you give to the nature that's closest to you.

* * *

There is a power that comes from organized effort in any peer group with the same intention. Unity is produced through the coordination of the efforts of two or more people working toward a definite end in a spirit of harmony. This is why the groups in Max Travel Club are normally kept small and intimate, because this is where magical moments take place, unlike a huge commercial travel event. There is no ego involved here where we're trying to be the biggest travel club in the world, because that's not necessary to make a bigger impact. Change comes from knowing the deeper self, and modern scientific research like Dr. Hawkins' proves how powerful a smaller group can be.

"One individual who lives and vibrates to the energy of optimism and a willingness to be nonjudgmental of others," he says, "will counterbalance the negativity of 90,000 individuals who calibrate at the lower weakening levels." Now imagine what a travel club with around twenty members per trip could do at the peak of the high energy field! Absolutely unstoppable, right? Not one person but twenty! When Alexander the Great went to conquer the Persian Empire, the king of Persia laughed when he heard how few Greek soldiers had come to fight. But it was Alexander who was laughing in the end. (I can hear a lot of my old fraternity brothers cheering and screaming right now, saying, "Yeah!" but that's beside the point.) It was the Persian king's ego that was laughing, and the ego is a negative energy field because it's not really who you are. The ego leads to suffering, as the Persian Empire learned to its peril.

Napoleon Hill said, "Man's brain may be compared to an electric battery. It is a well-known fact that a group of electric batteries will provide energy in proportion to the number and capacity of the cells it contains. A group of brains connected in a spirit of harmony will provide more thought energy than a single brain." This is where immersion happens: it's in these energy fields that you know and do more in your life within twelve months then you did the last twelve years. This is called change, a transformation that connects you to your essence, allowing you to realize that there really are no limits and you can create your own world. The increased energy created through this alliance becomes available to every individual brain in the group.

Whether you're traveling with our friendly and positive group in Max Travel Club or by yourself, with your spouse or significant other, or with a friend, you're taking your most valuable asset—time—and aligning it with success. As the world becomes more aware and conscious of its own fight for survival, and we raise our kids as if we're raising our grandkids, there needs to be a new meaning behind the word "vacation" and in the purpose of our travels.

This is not a war against sex, drugs, or rock 'n roll because we've all been there—never drugs with me, but I've learned not to judge anyone. My approach to travel means realizing you can have the time of your life without chemicals and the side effects of a chaotic night when you wake the morning after. I still party and go out *once in a while* myself, but you'll never see me in a bar on a Wednesday night, for example, unless it's a celebration of some sort, or I have a date I couldn't manage to schedule on the weekend. I'm not perfect, so I'm just like you: my awakening is still going through a growth process. I'm not some guru who knows it all. What I do know is what I want, and I know I want to share this journey with you and for you to be my travel buddy.

If you don't know what *you* want, I promise that you will either find it here or get much closer to it!

I personally believe that travel is an absolutely necessary psychological motivator that pushes you and gets you going again. It makes you more aware as you look at your life as the third person or observer. You will naturally see yourself explaining who you are, where you're going, and where you're coming from. Unitarian-Universalist minister Sarah York advocates travel, saying, "I recommend leaving. As long as you are in your home, something in your space will lure you into ordinary time."

Anybody attracted to these vacations for the soul is bright. That's why I would enjoy traveling with such individuals, as I know we are of like mind and can share a stimulating conversation. Napoleon Hill explains the benefits of such conversation thus: "If I give you one of my dollars in return for one of yours, each of us will have no more than we started with, but if I give you a thought in return for one of your thoughts, each of us will have gained a hundred percent dividend on his investment in time. No form of human relationship is as profitable as the exchange of useful thoughts."

Time is our most valuable asset. Whom do you spend time talking to and being around for hours and years of your life? My purpose in writing this book is to attract the right people in my life, not to make millions. I'll let the universe take care of that for me by following its proven principles.

I read an article recently that said only 2% of Americans have passports! Whether America is still considered the greatest nation on earth or not, even when the U.S. was solidly one of the most remarkable nations on Earth and the economy was at its strongest, still only 2% of Americans had passports. How preposterous! Wouldn't you think that as the most outstanding nation on Earth we would want to travel more and learn more about other cultures? The world is becoming smaller, and we must learn and grow with each other. My friends, whatever your nationality, culture, or religion, I invite you to join me, because no matter your background, we all have the same needs. It's time to jump out of our bubbles and grow for the survival of the human race, of all living beings—of the world.

"Our doubts are traitors, and make us lose the good we oft might win by fearing to attempt," William Shakespeare wrote. Changing your life isn't about performing a specific task, being in a certain occupation, or living in a particular location. It's about giving yourself in a creative and kind way that comes from your heart, using the skills and interests that are inherently part of you. Whatever skills you decide to learn through travel will become a part of you forever.

CHAPTER 3

MAX TRAVEL CLUB:

A Mutual Admiration Travel Society,
   Opening Doors to Places You Didn't Know Existed

Max Travel Club is the new paradigm of travel because it will answer the needs of spiritual seekers. The purpose of the transformations and growth that happen in this travel club is to create a flourishing society in which as many people as possible have wonderful lives filled with freedom, happiness, and fulfillment. This is where people outgrow their old belief systems like butterflies leaving their cocoons. Arriving at this placeless place, you experience moments of transition between who you *were* moving into who you *are*. All of you are in this place right now.

"From the dust of the earth to a human being there are a thousand steps," said Rumi, the great Sufi saint. "I have been with you through these steps. I have held your hand and walked by your side. You may think that I have left you on the side of the road. Don't complain, don't become mad, don't open the lid of the pot. Boil happily and be patient, remember what you're being prepared for." Every vacation with this club is a pilgrimage, a gathering, so much more than a workshop or seminar. A pilgrimage is somewhere people go to be transformed so that they will never be the same, so they will emerge different, shifted. You are not here for just another vacation, you are here for the great shift. You are a part of this great shift, and it's your responsibility to remind yourself of why you're really taking a vacation that can transform your life the way you desire most.

You are coming to experience the power of transformation, to reignite your awakening process, and we come together to remember and to remind ourselves of why we're really doing this: to remember the power of consciousness, to make the change we want possible, and to remember we are not alone in creating this great shift together. Deciding to join us is a catalyst that speeds the process of enlightenment.

The shift is occurring right now as you're reading this, and the transition of taking the vacation with Max Travel Club will save you years of time from contraction to expansion, from limitation to possibility, from fear to focus, from confusion to clarity, from small to huge, from forgetting to remembering. You join us to remember who you are and why you're still here on this planet at this time. When there is such a transformation happening, why not speed your process when possible? If you're still reading, this is your calling, the one you've felt all your life, whether you were aware of it or not. You have felt different, you've felt wisdom; you've longed for happiness for yourself and others around you. Travel is an environment where vision, love, inspiration, and healing take place. The world is in desperate need of your transformation for its own survival, not just yours.

Never disqualify yourself from life or this club because of anything you've gone through. Anything you've thought of as failures in your life are actually your qualifications. You're qualified and prequalified to do everything you're meant to do.

* * *

The purpose of this travel club is to heal, inspire, and uplift millions of souls to be shifted and changed.

*　*　*

Max Travel Club can be the catalyst to help you make two very important discoveries in your life. First, you will discover that your purpose is not as much about what you do as it is about how you feel. Your second discovery will be that feeling purposeful activates a power from your source to create anything that's consistent in all the areas of your life—spiritually, mentally, emotionally, physically, in your relationships, and of course financially.

For the mascot of Max Travel Club, I chose a raccoon, much like Walt Disney who chose a mouse. I chose a raccoon because a raccoon has self-respect. There's no raccoon out there who believes himself unworthy of what he intends to have. The raccoon is what it is and he doesn't think he is less valuable or short of being just because most humans don't value him. If the raccoon had no self-respect, he would simply die by acting on the basis of his own doubt that he is worthy of food, shelter, and whatever else raccoons desire. Respecting yourself should be a natural state for you to be in, just as it is for all of the animal kingdom. If you believe you're whole and perfect as you were created, Max Travel Club is your home. If you have some inner conflicts, you are sure going to be in a peer group that will hold you to a higher standard. Then eventually you won't wonder if you love yourself, you'll know that you do. And that will be an awakening, my friend.

Walt Disney died right before the Disney theme park opened. On the day of the opening, some negative reporter (who surely wouldn't belong in our club), said to Walt's brother, Roy, "This must be a bittersweet day for you." Roy Disney looked around and said, "Are you kidding? This is the most amazing day. The rides are working, there's beautiful weather, the kids are having a ball." "Yeah, but Walt wasn't here to see all this," the reporter pointed out. Roy replied, "Walt saw this before any of us saw this, and that's why you get to see all this."

You become what you think about most. You create what you visualize in your head, for the positive or negative, and your friends and associates play a big part in what you think about, so choose them wisely. I like to take leisure vacations once in a while with friends and family, although being completely aware that after the vacation nothing will change and my life will go back to normal. I look at it how most people do who work their whole lives and have nothing to show for it. The same goes with the way the majority takes a vacation: they have nothing that stays with them other than the picture on their Facebook page, which is forgotten about a week or two after the upload. When I take a traditional vacation, I just let my mind relax and have the time of my life, which is also okay. I don't mean to be judgmental if this is the typical vacation scenario for you. But you can get so much more! You can get all that plus grow in every area of your life. Imagine if you changed one area of your life or expanded upon it every time you took a vacation. You would be a completely different person after every vacation, being transformed every step of the way.

You have appointments with dozens, hundreds of people in the world. Why not make one with yourself through a life-changing vacation? We are human *beings*, not human *doings*, and therefore we must take some time and just *be*—like a vacation where you're totally enjoying every present moment and when you fall asleep, you're gone.

There will be times when we get together and allow ourselves to be entertained. Is just being entertained really your prerogative when there is now added value to what you used to call a vacation or entertainment?

People are using the internet to connect, but even if you connect online, like on Facebook for example, we still need the visceral experience of being together for connection.

I use to travel the world and experience amazing things, having the time of my life but still coming back home empty, wondering why life was what it was and not more. The emptiness came from ignoring certain conflicts in my life, unresolved relationships, and not listening to my heart's desire. I had the opportunity to stay in Amsterdam with my aunt Pam, start a new life there and go to college, but I was too scared to step out of my box and start somewhere new because I didn't know that opportunity lies in the unknown. Humans are creatures of habit, so I unhappily went back to my comfort zone, which was Santa Monica, California. Truthfully, I was running away from the realities of my life by traveling. I'd ask myself why I had to come back, why I couldn't have stayed where I was with my new friends and my new family on the other side of the world. I didn't realize that wherever I was, I would've felt the same emptiness inside because true beauty comes from the journey, realizing that wherever you lay your head is your home, because you're content and at peace with what is. No amount of wishing and dreaming will change your life, but new decisions will. Welcome to that journey, my friends. Welcome to Max Travel Club, where your whole world changes.

CHAPTER 4

HOLISTIC TRAVEL

"Tourists don't know where they've been; travelers don't know where they're going."

—Henry David Thoreau

"The tragedy of life is not so much what men suffer, but rather what they miss."

—Thomas Carlyle

Holistic vacations are meant to enhance your physical, emotional, mental, and spiritual well-being. Max Travel Club trips will have a focus on healing your body while addressing your physical health such that you achieve optimal health. The spiritual vacations will focus more on walking as you meditate, or improving your nutritional practice. Along with this, you will find that your entire mind, body, and soul will begin to transform. Activities with Max Travel Club will promote your physical, spiritual, and even social well-being. These approaches involve a variety of philosophies and techniques.

If you can't spend a full week, even a weekend holistic retreat can make a significant change in your life. The holistic centers give you an infinite number of possibilities for your future as you learn new skills and gain new perspectives. For example, the power of touch through massage will make you more aware of the effects of emotions on your physical health. Many religious leaders and health counselors use this to promote healing.

* * *

Are you a high achiever who's sacrificing your personal needs? Is your success contributing to a wholesome, fulfilled life? Is success worth the price you're paying? A holistic vacation will give you time to look at your life, who you are and what you are doing.

It amazes me how many people think a holistic vacation is a waste of time when they're not even marching to their own drumbeat. If you want a happy life in which you feel complete, you need to find your own personal rhythm, and when you're always on the go, you never have time to be aware of it. Bright, successful, and industrious people can get out of harmony with themselves—their body, their psyche, and their spiritual rhythm. When our bodies are not balanced and we are not in harmony, we are less effective, and everything seems to take more time, effort, and energy.

These vacations take place all over the world, maybe even close to where you live. For example, let's say you went on a women-only holistic vacation to Alaska. You would not only experience profound sightseeing opportunities, you would also learn to address yourself through sound, movement, art, bodywork, and meditation. Some of the many ways you might work to bring your body towards greater balance and centering are African dance, movement therapy, polarity energy exercises, neuromuscular therapy, Reiki, sound healing, storytelling, ceremony, music, art, movement, and stillness, all while experiencing the wonders, history, people, and wildlife of Alaska. Some like to visit Alaska's far north, where the summer sun never sets and it's ancient and historic. The Arctic Wildlife National Refuge is here, not to mention the western Arctic and the city of Nome, where some women have said they forget about the inconveniences of their old lives and start anew, completely connected to their spirits by feeding their souls. Peace is found at the end of the rainbow in the wilds of Alaska, places like Fairbanks and Denali National Park, even driving along the highway on the interior of Alaska.

If you're looking for wild Alaskan adventure, south-central Alaska is for you. Prince William Sound is my favorite, a place where you see glaciers break into the water and whales swim in the icy waves. Cooper River and Mat-Su Valley have a peaceful, country feel to them. After being introduced to the process of self-exploration, you will find the experience of visiting a remote location in Alaska's rugged southwest to be even more rewarding. You will meet the native people of wild Alaska in places like Kodiak Island or the Pribilof Islands. Many go fishing in Alaska's peninsula, while vegetarians just relax and consume their own delicious meals. Katmai National Park is like watching Animal Planet live as you see the bears capture flying fish for a feast, or watch sea lions loll on their backs. There's just so much to see and become aware of internally and on the planet we call home.

For an experience that has helped thousands make powerful changes at home and at work, with a certain confidence that helps you walk more strongly into your future, imagine a self-discovery vacation that holds a number of workshops, retreats, and tours to New Mexico or even to fifty acres of woodland in New York City. Imagine learning how to create a healthy, balanced work life where you learn leadership skills. Learn how to tap into your creative process for maximum health through pottery, song, music, journaling, and theater. There are weekend singles retreats or couples retreats where you can return every three months to share your insights and discoveries from the previous months. Imagine whitewater rafting, drumming while the sun sets, journal writing, and meditation in New Mexico. It's also an investment in your team-building and leadership skills. Vegetarian meals are common.

A Big Sur vacation in northern California is always an enlightening experience, and it's not just the sound of the sea. Esalen is a leader in holistic vacations, and I lead small groups for a transforming experience that will commit you to being deeper, richer, and more connected to your enduring spirit. Words can't explain an experience or its contribution to the world.

An eight-day vacation in the winter can promote health, happiness, and positive change by your connecting with the circle of life like the Native Americans do. Wonderful places to experience this are San Salvador, the Bahamas, and Tulum, Mexico. Picture embracing yoga in Tulum—it's something within your reach, whether you are a beginner or advanced. Anyone can vacation in Mexico, but add in two glorious yoga sessions a day and you go way beyond rested and relaxed. You come home rejuvenated and inspired for action (karma yoga!). Practices focus on peaceful yet deep engagement and radical acceptance as the doorways to transformation open, leading to wise and compassionate involvement in the world around us. All the while, we'll bask in the magic of this retreat. These experiences come with joining Max Travel Club.

Consider rhythm explorations and drum-building in San Salvador Island, Bahamas, where you build your own drum and investigate the potentials of sound and rhythm. You will discover their inner rhythms as they connect to each other and with nature. This island is a real "sleeping beauty," a scenic refuge that is considered one of the best-kept secrets within the region. It is renowned for historical ruins, rolling hills, stunning coral reefs, and miles of sandy beaches. Christopher Columbus made his first landfall here on his historic voyage to the New World. Four separate monuments mark the exact spot where he came ashore on October 12, 1492.

* * *

Scotland offers incredible coastlines, diverse nature, forests, and wonderful little towns and villages, as well as the great city of Aberdeen. Here you'll learn spiritual practices to clarify your purpose and manifest "right living." We explore your unique way of opening to spiritual guidance to unveil your potential and bring benefit to yourself, your relationships, and the planet. We integrate spiritual healing practices with practical work and release disturbing patterns, converting them into energy to support your goals. All the while we explore numerous sightseeing opportunities, whatever tickles your fancy—zoos, aquariums, wildlife, museums, theme parks, parks and gardens, castles, art galleries, monuments, and historical buildings. These many tourist attractions give you the chance to browse delights you can savor during your visit.

The historic culture and sights in Scotland are phenomenal. Many tour companies can expose you to these, but only Max Travel specializes in helping you gain a deeper spiritual connection and develop your personal leadership skills, or focuses on inner and outer sustainability, spiritual ecology, and creativity. Max Travel experiences are far more enriching than just visiting a country. Activities after meditation cover a whole range of options from gentle to white-knuckle, including walking, climbing, cycling, horseback riding, angling, excursions, golfing, and extreme sports. Specialized activities like birdwatching and rambling clubs are available, and there are indoor activities for rainy days.

This journey within will use movement, sound, and breath to cleanse and balance your energy, express feelings, remove blocks, and connect you better with the flow of life and all that is, raising the vibration while giving you the experience of being a light-filled spirit in a body. Travels to the northeast of Scotland also offer opportunities for you to learn new tools that can easily be integrated into everyday life and that allow you to transform your inner landscape. You can create new neural pathways that bring about personal healing and contribute to the creation of a positive world for all. These practices release blocking beliefs and reconnect us with our unlimited potential to shine.

＊＊＊

One of the most magical places to take a vacation for your soul is Cortes Island in British Columbia, where you'll find forty-eight acres of forest, beachfront, gardens, and orchards. The island is known for its rich marine life, including sea lions, otters, and porpoises. It's also home to more than 220 species of birds and forests full of firs, cedars, pines, maples, wild berries, mushrooms, and wildflowers. You can enjoy and benefit from the amenities on this sacred island without needing to take a special workshop.

Extracurricular activities include yoga, meditation, massage and body care, kayak and sailing trips, reflexology, and acupressure. A Cortes Island naturalist leads morning bird walks, evening owling expeditions, tidal tours, stargazing, cruises, tours of archaeological sites, and a garden tour. This vacation for the soul is complemented by splendid vegetarian and seafood cuisine.

An eco-tourism retreat center in Maui stands next to the ocean and boasts beautiful hiking trails and waterfall lagoons. A romantic setting only fifteen minutes from town, it offers sunrise views and optional yoga and meditation classes. Love shows itself in every detail and living being in your environment here.

CHAPTER 5

SPIRITUAL VACATIONS FOR THE SOUL

"Ships are the nearest things to dreams that hands have ever made, for somewhere deep in their oaken hearts the soul of a song is laid."

—ROBERT N. ROSE, FROM THE POEM "SHIPS"

"Who you are is neverending, who you are is everlasting, who you are is spirit."

—DR. WAYNE DYER

"How spiritual you are has nothing to do with what you believe, but everything to do with your state of consciousness."

—ECKHART TOLLE

One of the best things you can do for your spirit is to head out and get away from where you are. This can be something as simple as spending a week on the beach or taking a break in the mountains. These places are known to help you reduce your stress and help you to relax again. Unfortunately, they are also short-lived solutions. Within a few days of your normal routine, you will find that all the benefits you earned on vacation have been lost.

In this chapter, we take a look at a series of Max Travel Club experiences that offer lasting spiritual benefits. If you choose to travel with me on such vacations, you will not only be able to renew your spiritual focus, you will also find that your life is enriched. Each traveler will have a different approach. Some will be Buddhist, Christian, or Jewish, while others might be Sufi or New Age. You will find that some choices are cemented in simple meditation, while others invite you to focus on your community and the entire world. Each practice will help you to become more active in your search for spirituality and will travel with you back into your daily life.

You will have the opportunity of traveling with me to a series of retreats and centers that will help you address your spiritual concerns. These programs are designed to assist you through a number of different approaches. One might use a Quaker prayer, while another could focus on meditation or even the art of spiritual healing through touch. In some cases, you might find an isolated experience in which you make a pilgrimage to a sacred spot. The options are endless, as are the things you can take from each to enrich your entire life. You will come to understand some of the different ways you can add both spirituality and faith into your everyday life. Even if you're already solid in your spirituality, these activities and sacred sites can enhance your experience.

There is little doubt that most every child has had religious exposure in their life. This formal education in religion comes from their parents' choice of church, synagogue, or other place of worship. While many will continue with these religious practices, others will begin to seek out alternative choices. In some cases, a person might choose a different path that doesn't limit their schedule or life too much and still allows for their current path of life. Others still have no idea in what direction they should go to get the teaching and spiritual practices they desire.

If you are one of those people who is content with your spiritual journey, you will still find travel opportunities that meet your needs. But if you're like so many others who believe that something is missing in their lives, you will still find a vacation perfect for your spiritual focus. Such a vacation or retreat shouldn't be something you really need to think about, because it's more of an inner calling. Your spirit draws you to the retreat, just as your body calls out to you for rest. Your inner calling for such a vacation or retreat is nothing less than an invitation to a momentary or slight appearance of heaven in the average world.

Of course, this kind of vacation will also help you make better decisions in your life, along with rest and doing things you usually never have time to do. But ultimately our group of travelers is really coming into symmetry with a greater power than any other on earth. Expect to be changed and don't judge how small or large that change is; just know that it's a great gift.

In Max Travel Club, we don't always focus on travel to one place. No matter where we're going, our focus is concentrating on heightening awareness of our moods and feelings of the journey. It's about the experience itself and a deep attentiveness toward how it moves you. All I ask is that if you join the club and take part in our spiritual adventures, you'll look beyond other members' differences, because our personal goals are actually the same: *we all want to know how to live with purpose.*

Take every opportunity to ask yourself *why*. What else could this mean to every emotional response you feel? This is how I really realized the values that were driving my life—and yes, it was on a vacation. Not being able to go on a vacation is not an excuse to stay away from such questions. Wilderness is therapy because answers come to you much more easily in nature. You can become aware of the sacred sound of birds in the morning, the rich smell of the earth. Spend time with a flower. Did you know smelling a rose gives you twenty electrolytes of energy for free? I'm awed by the wonders of the world, and I hope I'm traveling till the day I die.

The main point of a spiritual vacation, retreat, adventure, pilgrimage, or voyage is to enhance your spiritual experience, whether you're after an inner journey to a new place within or a physical journey to a sacred place. Traveling in general is a spiritual practice for many because leaving your comfort zone puts you in the present moment at all times as you consistently experience new things and see new places. Sometimes you won't always know what's going to happen and you can't be completely in control, so you just have to accept the situation for what it is. Just remember that you're the experiencer, not the experience. In every experience there is a part of you that's still unchanged: the part of you without fear, because all fear comes from change, and you're being open to change just by traveling. Your consciousness shapes all forms of your destiny, your mind, body, and spirit, and if we learn to guide our consciousness, we can guide everything that we experience in life.

* * *

Dr. Deepak Chopra wrote, "The environment is your extended body. So you have your cosmic body and your personal body, and you have influence over it as much as you have influence over your personal body. If you can wiggle your toes with the flicker of an intention, you can do that with your cosmic body too." Another little story I love is one in which a reporter asked the Dalai Lama what was the greatest religion on Earth. "Any religion that makes you a better person," he replied. God, Allah, Buddha, Krishna, Tao, Jah—these are the sounds of creation.

It's time to become aware of our thoughts. I'm sure you've heard that our thoughts control our minds; that's because every thought you have has an energy that will either strengthen or weaken you. Understanding something is different from actually knowing it through experience. Once you become immersed in a spiritual program and enter society again, you'll know people can't bring you down if you're performing at the higher energies. Higher positive energies eat lower negative energies just like big fish eat little fish; darkness turns into light.

The values of a living culture and our travel club's living culture are service, joy, peace, harmony, compassion, nurturing, infinite possibility, faith, embrace of goodness, embrace of happiness, approval, support, and belief in the innocence of ourselves and others. This is a group culture that also supports the members in their successes, not their miseries. These vacations allow you to realize or expand upon the knowledge that you're a part of the universe and not separate from it. When you come to this realization, you realize that the more others succeed, the more you're capable of as well. You no longer see other people's successes as a threat.

Max Travel Club is about appreciating an anxiety-free vacation with spiritual awareness, and learning how to carry that back into your everyday life. These environments attract miracles, shifts in perception: you saw life one way, and after your trip you leave that behind. A spiritual vacation will make you much more aware of miracles so that you can attract them more often and come into self-realization.

* * *

On an exotic trip to Bali, you would learn how to move into the modern world without losing your sense of balance on Earth. This part of Indonesia has a way of creeping into your heart and creating symmetry with your soul. This is a perfect place for inner and outer exploration. The people on this island believe that the physical world is permeated by the spiritual world, *sekala niskala* ("visible invisible") and this is a great source of inspiration. You will get to talk with locals during an exclusive visit with mountain villagers. You will talk to them about health and healing practices through their spirituality. You will also enjoy Balinese music and Kecak dance at the Uluwatu Temple at sunset. You can also bathe in the Indian Ocean, which for some is like a baptism.

Nepal, Tibet, and Bhutan are the rooftop of the world, where you will feel your soul expanding. I also sometimes like Bhutan over Tibet for a spiritual vacation because Bhutan is free from commercialism. In Nepal and Tibet you can explore Eastern consciousness by meeting and studying with Buddhist nuns and monks. Your attention will be on how the sense of a new place affects human consciousness and raises your spirit. You will naturally catch yourself connecting to the cosmos with profound intensity.

Bangkok, Phuket, and Chaing Mai in Thailand are destinations offered through Max Travel Club. All three cities offer so much to see and do for eager visitors. Many elect Bangkok for their first choice, as it is vibrant and fascinating to see. Bangkok is the oldest of all the cities in Thailand, steeped in beautiful buildings and amazing culture. The numerous temples will entice you to wander through them, admiring the craftsmanship and beauty they hold. Two breathtaking sights you should not miss on your stop in Bangkok are the Emerald Buddha and the Grand Palace of the king of Thailand.

Experiencing the sandy golden beaches and crystal clear water in Phuket will keep you captivated for your stay. There are beachfront hotels and accommodations that are a mere stone's throw from the stunning beaches. Many of Max Travel Club's vacations for the soul allow you to spend a relaxing three days here before moving on to the next city. Although Chiang Mai is a lengthy thirteen-hour train journey from Bangkok, it offers a totally different side of Thailand and is well worth the trip.

* * *

"Beautiful things happen when change is ready to bloom," Carl Jung wrote. "Everything points in one direction and miracles seem to happen." It takes courage to rely on your intuition and take a vacation for the soul, but if you do, you encourage the kind of synchronicity Jung described.

I remember once being cursed by an obnoxious old woman when all I was doing was being nice from the bottom of my heart. In that moment I hated her; my ego was so offended, I hoped she would have a heart attack. After walking for five minutes I figured, what do I know about her situation? Why don't I just assume that she is a good person? That was a miracle: a week later she was crying on my shoulder, feeling horrible because the day I encountered her, her son had just died. She told me kids are supposed to bury their parents, not vice versa. Then I was hugging this random old lady who had offended me the previous week.

In general, when you catch yourself in moments of judgment and choose to focus on a person's innocence instead of guilt, or a person's capability instead of past mistakes, you experience a miracle. A spiritual vacation has so many benefits because the more miracles you have, the more you're able to apply them to yourself for inner peace. It is essential to invest in your enlightenment. Every cent or minute I've invested in mine, I've gotten back tenfold. Thomas Merton warned, "For if we live always and only under the pressure of others around us, of deadlines and obligations, our true self may get lost. When people are merely submerged in a mass of impersonal human beings pushed around by automatic forces, they lose their true humanity, their integrity, their ability to love, their capacity for self-determination." A vacation for the soul changes all that by reminding you whom you should be when you come back home. Poemen said, "Have the mentality of the stranger in the place where you live so you don't too readily express your opinions and you will be at peace." An overwhelmed mind has trouble absorbing anything, and therefore it is not healthy to wait until you reach this point before taking a vacation or getaway. And remember that a spiritual vacation or a vacation for the soul is not intended to impress someone else or to make you stronger to compete with another. It *can* make you stronger and impress others, yes, but if those things are your goals, then you're missing the whole point.

Vacationers can choose to learn meditation! Scientific evidence has proven that meditation can lower blood pressure levels, reduce chronic pain and anxiety, and increase intelligence-related tasks. Modern research also proves meditation as a tool for productivity and efficiency at work. When meditating while you travel, you withdraw your mind from everyday concerns so that it may come into contact with the divine. A professor of mine once said, "When you meditate, your conscious mind actually controls your automatic nervous system." Studies show improved cardiovascular health, understanding, awareness of time, happiness, and originality, as well as a strikingly bright and intense imagination and a greater capacity for love. Meditation strengthens your immune system to fight off disease. It creates brainwaves that make you relaxed to deeply relaxed after twenty minutes. Psychologists say that meditating in a group produces good fellowship that adds to your prosperity.

All the vacations in Max Travel Club offer nourishment for the mind, body, and spirit at diverse levels. Our trips that focus on healing the body and promoting physical health also address the mind and spirit by giving you necessary variety in your life and developing optimal attitudes. Vacations with spiritual emphasis don't ignore your body, either; there will be practices involving walking meditation or healthy nutritional practices. Even drumming can be a form of meditation. These vacations offer advancement for the transformation of your mind, body, and spirit.

Your membership will give you access to both large and small centers that provide all-inclusive programming. All offer activities that promote physical, emotional, mental, social, intellectual, and spiritual well-being. Their approach is as inclusive as their focus; techniques and philosophies are varied and interdisciplinary. A weekend or week at any of these places can result in significant changes in your life. Dedicated to promoting physical, emotional, and spiritual health and to facilitating personal as well as planetary transformation, the holistic centers offer infinite possibilities. There are a multitude of skills to be learned and perspectives to be gained. Whether the medium is Japanese wooden swordplay, guided imagery, journal-writing, or drum-building, you can discover something about yourself. You can learn to relax with biofeedback and stress management techniques. Physical fitness can be improved through tennis or yoga. Leisure interests can be developed in areas such as painting or poetry. Your career potential can be enhanced through workshops in management or communication skills. Intimacy can be taken to new heights through sexuality workshops. Spirituality can be discovered through Native American rituals, Tibetan chanting, or Judeo-Christian meditation techniques. Best of all, you don't have to confine yourself to just one area. Many of these programs offer opportunities to participate in myriad activities to truly integrate the mind, body, and spirit.

You can achieve anything if you follow certain laws. With no experience, two days after I graduated and during a recession, I closed a $30,000 commission in the mortgage industry with a complete stranger because that had been my goal for months. Sadly, I also missed my graduation party by constantly focusing on the future, never on the present moment. This led to major suffering because I wasn't happy. I was missing out on life. Success is only one part of life. There is no point in success without fulfillment. A holistic vacation reminding me that success without fulfillment equals failure was absolutely necessary and fulfilling. Take a vacation while learning the art of fulfillment—now you're at the top of the ladder, my friend. How you *feel* is your life! What you do and accomplish is not your life, it's not who you are.

A vacation is supposed to make you feel good, and a holistic vacation does so much more than that. If you listen to the lyrics of Bruno Mars' "Billionaire," it's really easy to see that the singer wants to be rich because he thinks it will make him feel good. Why wait till you're a billionaire—why not just feel good now? That makes the wealth-building process so much more enjoyable anyway. On a spiritual vacation, you will be led by spiritual intuition, rather than limited by your emotional fear. Perhaps Muhammed said it best: "Do not tell me how educated you are, tell me how much you have traveled."

CHAPTER 6

THE WORLD IS OURS: VACATIONS TO GIVE BACK

"The purpose of life is to give, the purpose of life is to enrich the lives of others in some way. The measure of your life will not be in the duration of your life, it will be measured in the donations of your life."—Dr. Wayne Dyer

In order for your mind, body, and spirit to be in balance, you need to contribute. Contribution brings purpose to your life and really pushes you to grow spiritually, emotionally, mentally, physically, in your relationships, and financially.

While some vacations that require you to contribute can make you feel a little tense, they will also help you to get beyond yourself. Maybe it will include helping to build a home for someone without one, cleaning up an area to better the environment, teaching English as a second language, going on a walk for peace, or even helping track wolves, which is my favorite. However, for a period of time, you'll be doing something that makes a difference. When you work to make a difference in the world around you, you'll be surprised that it's your own life that ends up seeing the biggest difference.

Once you return to your regular schedule, you'll have a new faith in your ability to offer contributions to the world around you, to nature and to the human race. This vacation will help you build commitment and will provide you with a vision to continue working for causes that you really believe in today. When you have this experience, you'll quickly realize what things are really of importance in your life. Suddenly those stresses in your life may not seem so big as you begin applying yourself to something that is far bigger than you.

Service is what helps you feel on purpose; giving is what fills in the emptiness. How so? Every religious and spiritual leader knows you're born with nothing and you leave with nothing. Therefore, the purpose of life must then be in giving, which is what fills the soul and brings us closer to creation.

I know it's a difficult task for many to grasp. "Action and service towards others and to my planet? But I'm already so busy!" is what most say. If you think from the end, whether it's your goals being accomplished or you being on your deathbed, you will realize that nobody, absolutely nobody, wishes they'd spent more time in the office taking care of business. At the end of our lives, it's the *moments* we remember because we won't remember everything. There will be many of those moments created through Max Travel Club.

Science supports the benefit of giving. According to Dr. Hawkins, "Research has shown that a simple act of kindness directed towards another improves the functioning of the immune system and stimulates the production of serotonin in both the recipient of the kindness and the person extending the kindness, or even to a third party watching."

James Allen said, "The dreamers are the saviors of the world, so be a dreamer."

When you offer from the heart, to help others in times of need, know that you are helping yourself.

CHAPTER 7

HEALTH IS WEALTH AND HEALING VACATIONS FOR THE SOUL

Do you realize how beneficial vacations can be to your health? It doesn't matter if you're dealing with physical ailments or mental stress, they can both be relieved with a much-needed vacation. Once you experience it, you will see everyone's attitudes improving. However, the effects always seem to be short-lived. So even though it was great while it lasted, it was really only a short-term escape.

To make them last over a long-term period, you have to find the right vacations that actually promote healing. Even though you won't be able to eliminate your past suffering, gaining the skills and knowledge about promoting health will allow you to deal with all problems in a better way. In the end, you're just more comfortable.

Keep in mind you don't have to have a major medical issue or mental crisis for these vacations to be beneficial. Sometimes they are needed when a person has gone through a traumatic illness and survived. There are others who just want to improve their well-being. Whatever the case may be, healing vacations are perfect for everyone.

In the beginning, it's the mind and spirit that are the main focus. A vacation is designed to promote emotional healing. It's important to understand that these are not mutually exclusive. Mind and spirit programs provide physical practices like proper breathing. There are times, however, when these are set up to address the emotional impact of a physical illness. It's also possible for a program to help the body utilize both mental and spiritual practices. A good example of this would be something like meditation.

In the end, health-promoting vacations are all about organization of the mind, body, and soul. Finding the right vacation for your particular needs is right around the corner.

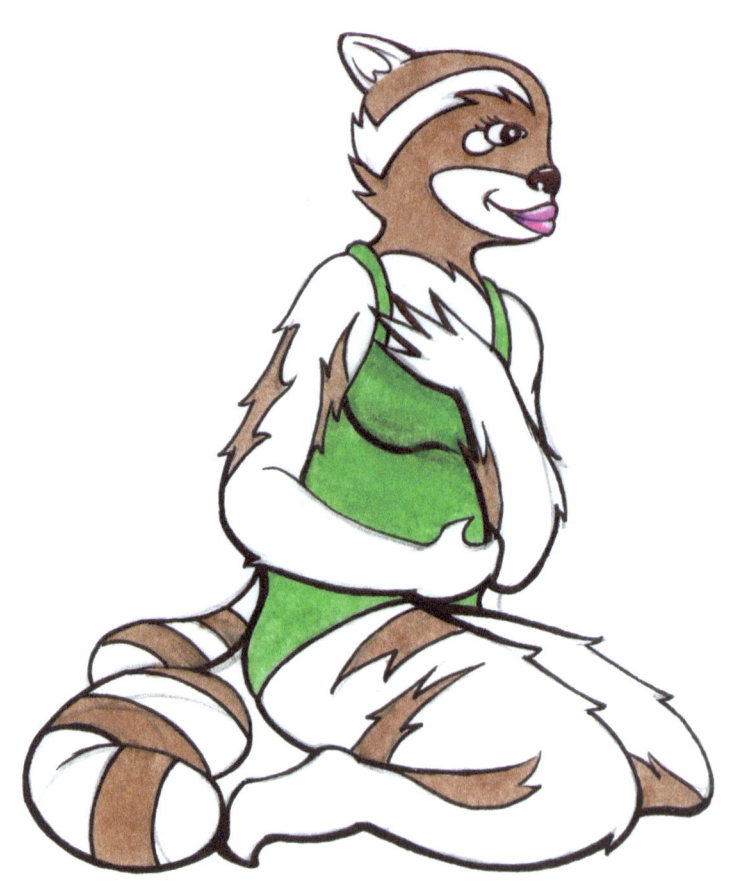

CHAPTER 8

VACATIONS THAT HEAL THE SOUL

"When I look back it seems to me all the grief that had to be, left me when the pain sore, stronger than I was before."

—NORMAN COUSINS

"All disease comes from a state of unforgiveness."

—COURSE OF MIRACLES

"Forgiving and releasing resentment will dissolve even cancer."

—LOUISE L. HAY

Vacations for healing the soul are for anybody who has been neglecting their needs. This is usually due to a busy schedule. Stress has such a negative impact on our overall health. Anxiety and headaches are caused by stress, and if you don't take the time to heal, it will eventually hurt your immune system and lead to high blood pressure, heart disease, and so on. The National Institutes of Health recommend alternative and holistic healing therapies over conventional medicine for treating stress. Max Travel Club's vacations for healing the soul can help you reverse stress-related health problems and prevent them too.

"Our bodies are not designed to become ill—they are designed to heal and become healthy," writes Dr. Deepak Chopra. "It is up to us to walk that road and to honor our whole being. A healthy being is a healthy body, mind, and spirit." These vacations are about reconnecting with the healer within you so you can maintain lifelong vitality. They will make you more committed to making positive changes in your life. They are real journeys in which there are no quick fixes and cure-alls.

You can make your experience match your needs, but I'm personally adventurous, so I've hiked past remote Hawaiian lagoons and rare wild orchids, kayaked amongst sea turtles bigger than I am, and taken a helicopter ride to the top of a volcano, all while learning yogic breath work and eating a vegetarian diet of local fruits and vegetables. Whatever kind of retreat you choose, you'll learn how to maintain your health by moving towards a better quality of life. Your decision to join will have an effect on more than just you and your loved ones. As Louise L. Hay said, "First we heal ourselves, then our family, then the planet."

Many successful businesspeople live by a sort of heartless philosophy in which responsibilities must be attended to no matter what else is going on. "Even on the morning after his wife's death, the farmer still had to milk the cows," they might say. I understand that the world won't stop for anybody, but psychologists tell us that every loss invokes deep memories of our infantile separation from our mothers. Healing from loss should be taken seriously if it affects you negatively. A healing vacation for the soul will be necessary, even if you think you're strong enough.

* * *

Modern Science and Health

Next time you're bored and tempted to turn on the TV, try this technique I've found useful. Just get comfortable and clear your mind of any thoughts. If they do creep in, don't react to them; just notice them and let them go. See if you can go for five full minutes, and observe how you feel. Further, when you quiet your mind, you can make far better use of your intuition, which will lead you out of the ruts and into places you may not have realized you wanted to go.

Drinking plenty of liquids *before* you're dehydrated is the way to health, not just because it stops the hunger pangs, but because a fully liquidated body keeps diseases away. Water can heal the damages of stress, since the side effects of stress are a reaction that comes after stress eats your insides up like a worm. Water is necessary to break up the food you eat so it can be digested more easily and plays a big part in metabolism. We drink so much soda or juice with our food, as if that can replace the water we need. But soda dehydrates you, removing the water you previously had in your system, making the situation worse. Dehydration can occur before you recognize it. Just because you have a dry mouth does not mean you're dehydrated, and lacking a dry mouth doesn't mean you *aren't* dehydrated. When your urine is yellow, that is a sign of some dehydration. Keep in mind that alcohol and coffee can produce pale urine, so that may fool you into thinking you're hydrated. This is because coffee gets rid of more water in your body than is contained in the coffee itself. Caffeine even opens up your pores, leading to sweaty hands.

A 200-pound person needs 100 ounces of water throughout the day. I used to think there were reservoirs in the body that stored water, but this is simply not true. Whatever we drink gets circulated, collects the toxic waste, and hydrates areas that need it. Dr. Batmanghel advises, "Every two to three hours we should be drinking two to three glasses of water, or else the body will become dehydrated. First thing in the morning we need more water because we've been in bed for about eight hours without drinking. First thing in the morning is when your body is most dehydrated."

Modern science is not the first to emphasize adequate hydration. Ayurveda, the ancient, traditional medicine practiced in India, advises drinking warm water in the morning because it strengthens your digestive power and reduces metabolic waste. It's the frequency of drinking water, rather than the quantity, that ayurvedic medicine considers important. On the other hand, cold water is said to increase vitality and strength, tone muscle, and aid in digestion. Hot water lessens pain, frees you from abnormal clogging of internal organs, releases toxins through perspiration, calms the body, and frees you from spiritual tension.

For those of you who are confused, test both methods and see what works best with your body. The point here is to *drink water regardless* and don't let these two different studies confuse you, because the power is not in knowing, *the power is in doing*. Drink water *every single* morning after you wake up and go to the bathroom. When we're dehydrated our blood pressure rises, but at the same time we don't want to overdo it and flush all the good stuff out of our system. Eating ample vegetables and greens puts those lost minerals back in your system. It's a beautiful, never ending cycle, my friend. You have to stay aware of your body, which is something you learn on a vacation for the soul. Not being able to wake up early in the morning and being depressed is also a sign of dehydration. Water is a main energizer in the body, and it's difficult to get to the higher energy levels without it because it produces hydroelectric energy at the cells' membranes, particularly in the nervous system, which controls brain function. These cells of ours continually communicate with each other and need a lot of energy, and they rely on the energy that comes from water.

Many scientists with traditional training believe that cravings for alcohol and soda are also a sign of dehydration. Even sickness during pregnancy is a sign of dehydration. Allergies, asthma, hypertension, and diabetes are all signs of dehydration. My heartburn and chest pains were signs of dehydration. When I used to drink four to six Red Bulls before an exam, my body actually became exhausted and couldn't focus on the test because all that caffeine and sugar had sucked out the water in my system, as if I were taking an exam in the middle of the desert. Most muscle or physical pains are a sign of dehydration. Our lungs shut down gradually when there is a lack of water in our system, and obviously breathlessness and breathing problems come with that. High cholesterol and chronic fatigue come from a lack of water; cholesterol is something the body manufactures when it needs it. Osteoperosis, cancer—these are all due to dehydration.

The big corporations selling medicine and pills do not support a vacation that can take you to another level. They do not want you to benefit from a life-changing vacation through Max Travel Club, because they want you to be sick. Sick people bring corporations their profits; healthy people do not. All my club members want the truth, and they know they have a higher value, even if the big corporations selling medicine only see them as a good source of income. Growing in consciousness and being wiser is the only way to live a healthy and blessed life, and we must stick together.

I was stunned by what I read in Dr. Gary Null et al.'s book *Death by Medicine*, which provides shocking statistics about the state of health and wellness in America:

> The number of people having in-hospital, adverse reactions to prescribed drugs is 2.2 million per year. The number of unnecessary antibiotics prescribed annually for viral infections is 20 million per year. The number of unnecessary medical and surgical procedures performed annually is 7.5 million per year. The number of people exposed to unnecessary hospitalization annually is 8.9 million per year.
>
> The most stunning statistic, however, is that the total number of deaths caused by conventional medicine is an astounding 783,936 per year. It is now evident that the American medical system is the leading cause of death and injury in the U.S. (By contrast, the number of deaths attributable to heart disease in 2001 was 699,697, while the number of deaths attributable to cancer was 553,251.5).
>
> By exposing these gruesome statistics in painstaking detail, we provide a basis for competent and compassionate medical professionals to recognize the inadequacies of today's system and at least attempt to institute meaningful reforms.

Ayurveda shows us that we have missed out on a few billion years of experience because our bodies are pharmacies that produce more drugs than what is at the drugstore, and the body's drugs are better quality because they're natural. Learning to heal naturally will benefit us and the next generation. Through our minds and bodies, we create the world we live in, and so we have infinite choices of whether we want to be healed or not. Right now you have a million atoms in your body that were once in the body of Christ or Buddha or Michelangelo or Joan of Arc. Your body has a wealth of intelligence. You have a new body once a year; you make new skin once a month; you get a new stomach lining every five days. You don't even have the same brain cells you had a year ago.

We are at a stage where ideas are becoming the revolutionary force, rather than genes. Whatever you feel immediately becomes your biochemical reality. When you place a meaning on an experience—for example, identifying something as a peaceful and calm experience—you produce a molecule that's more beneficial to the immune system than any drug on the market. You create these molecules every second of your existence, so stay aware of what you focus on and the meanings behind the events that take place in your life. If you think you're going to die, your body might just listen to that message.

Ayruveda masters have taught me that the solution to healing is to consistently expose myself and seek the unknown in every moment of my life, because that is where the opportunity is. And since the purpose of life is happiness, we must continue to step into the unknown to remain happy, since that's when we're consistently growing as human and spiritual beings. So basically we know that the box we're so scared to leave is the real trap, because there is no growth in staying in a place that is familiar and comfortable. Work and career stress can confine us to these boxes like nothing else. More people die on Monday at 9 a.m. than at any other time of the week. One of the main reasons for heart disease is job dissatisfaction, or people who have no meaning and purpose in their lives and are just waiting for retirement.

The book *A Course in Miracles*, published by the Foundation for Inner Peace, states that fear is to love as darkness is to light. This means that fear is the absence of love. Where love is present, fear cannot exist.

CHAPTER 9

HEALTH-PROMOTING VACATIONS

"We create the mind, we are not the mind; we create the body, and through our mind and our body we ultimately create the experience of this world."

—Dr. Deepak Chopra

Your body is often a reflection of your view of life. People who are healthy weren't just born that way. There is a pattern in the way they think and act. One out of two people in America die of heart disease, and one in three dies from cancer. In the Max Travel Club, we are separate and distinguish ourselves from this category. Instead of focusing on disease, we address the source of the problem, often treating it before it happens. Even if you're already fighting disease, you will learn to deal with the problem's source, rather than doing what the majority of victims do, which is to keep treating the problem. (I myself refuse to be called a victim no matter what I've been through, because that takes away my power.) I'm here to live life to the fullest, and none of us can manage that if our health is at risk. We consume an average of 285 grams of sugar a day, but we should reduce that to 20 grams. Even milk has sugar, which makes sense—it's designed to help a sixty-pound calf grow into a two-thousand-pound cow. Unsweetened almond milk is a better choice. Eliminate sugar and practice meditation.

My mentor/travel buddy, Kumar, who studied at Harvard Medical School, said research makes it clear that germs are not the source of disease. He explained, "You can have all these germs in your body and not have the disease they are supposed to cause, and you also can have a disease when those germs aren't present." Hearing this shocked me and made me feel as if I were in the twilight zone. "Germs are a sign of life," he went on. "If you create an environment that's polluted, germs are going to magnify. So they keep feeding, cloning, and producing more of themselves." Don't take advice from unhealthy people, many of whom don't even know they are unhealthy. If your friends are unhealthy, they won't respect your standards for a higher level of nourishment. Once you realize that your body is driven by your mind and spirit, you will laugh at the folly of it all. Advertisements, endorsements, medications won't have any effect on you. In the Max Travel Club, you will be with healthy and admirable people.

Your principles of health directly affect the things you say or do. It's your principles that allow you to carefully select what you put in your body, or affect how you cope with disease. The choices you make now will affect your physical and emotional destiny.

Stress communicates nervous energy to our cells and eats our insides up like worms. You want to come back from a vacation balanced. Stress is an electrical imbalance on the body due to our biochemistry, and this imbalance messes up our cells, which messes up our organs, which pretty much messes up your life.

Acid in our bodies breaks down our positive biochemistry. Sugar that doesn't come from fruit turns into acid. Coffee, alcohol, even pizza converts to acid. The processed cheese on pizza is acidic, the crust contains sugar, and so does the pepperoni. Frustration, anger, and resentment also create acid. These are the emotions that put me in the emergency room three times, even though I tried to blame it on something else. Laughter therapy had a phenomenal effect on my health and my wallet. I'm not hooked up to an IV anymore; I'd rather watch eight hours of comedies and be good. Friends who are clowns and don't take life seriously contribute to society without knowing it. You can boost your immune system and your endorphins through laughter. This isn't about making jokes that put other people down; acts of kindness have been proven to boost your immune system. So people who tell street jokes for some reason don't seem to live too long—I haven't met any old men telling street jokes. If I see it on TV I'll laugh, but not in real life.

I do exercises I enjoy without putting any stress on myself, because working out under stress can do more damage than good. Shifting my mindset from seeing running by the beach as a duty to it being a gift allowed me to run more and actually feel less tired. I dropped my ego and connected to the source. The same source that helped Lance Armstrong win the Tour de France is the same source flowing through every human being. The challenge is connecting to it. The best way is to learn on vacation getaway without the stress and day-to-day chaos. Once you experience such a vacation, you will realize that nothing tastes as good as fit, healthy, and vital feels. These special vacations will get you addicted to that feeling, and it will change every aspect of your life—your relationships, your finances, everything. It's sad to know that we value everything more than our bodies: money, career, anything to keep our significant other from complaining, but our bodies are our last priority. My grandfather was different. He made his body his first priority, and he lived to 112 years of age.

Again, Earl Nightingale advised, "If you want to be successful, do the opposite of what the majority is doing." That's exactly what I do. I no longer associate with friends who don't respect the way I respect my body. My peer group is at another level now. My best friend is at the number-one grad school for his major, and he's training for the Olympics. At Max Travel Club, you will be accepted, not criticized, for your higher standards.

Nutrition without proper digestion and absorption is equal to having no nutrition. All the toxins, acids, and yeast in your body consume your nutrition. Lots of fruit is great as long as we don't consume too many processed foods, because processed foods are sugar and we'd only be creating more acids. What got me into all this research is my dentist telling me that it's not the sugar from the chocolates and candy that are burning holes in my teeth, it's the sugar that turns into acid. I even saw a program on KCET, a California community television station, explaining that acid settles in the weakest part of your body, make it worse. We must take away food that doesn't provide enough energy. I love steak, but it sure does leave me at an energy deficit where I can't do anything but go to sleep, because I'm putting a dead animal into my body with no electrical charges.

Cooked oils also create an acidic environment that takes away more energy than it gives. We age a lot more quickly with a bad diet. Snacks like almonds and cucumbers, green drinks like wheatgrass—these are what get us going and make us look younger than our age. Eating fruits, cutting out the processed foods, and being around nature and flowers also provide energy that scientists have measured. Think about it: being around a smoggy environment decreases your energy level.

Negative thoughts, words, and actions poison and unbalance our bloodstream. Even being in front of your computer for too long can create an imbalance in your blood due to radiation. That's why I have a mini cactus by my computer, because a cactus absorbs radiation. Anything that is imbalanced weakens, dies, or mutates, which means that your cells become disorganized. Similarly, every time you have a negative thought, your body is misaligned from your mind.

It's the environment you create in your body that brings the little creatures and yeast to eat all your sugar and then protein. The creatures in your body make you want to eat more sweets. IT'S ALWAYS THE ENVIRONMENT. You can make it a positive one by sticking to greens. Same thing goes with your external world: you create your outside world just like you create your internal one, and since the internal reflects the external and the type of people you attract, you know the journey begins within. I myself am only trying to attract people who take me to a higher level in life. The same should go for you and the club you associate with.

Sugar equals acid and acid equals the glue that makes your red blood cells stick together in an unhealthy way. If you can get tested, you can see how your cells are misshapen. To figure the level of acid in your body, you can take a pH of water test at your local drugstore, or order a pH litmus paper and booklet online. If you're below the 7.0 water balance, you have to make a revolutionary change in your diet. If you're at a 7.45, you have healthy blood. If you're at a 7.5, cancer cells are dormant and completely inactive. If you manage to get to a pH level of 8.5, you will literally kill cancer.

CHAPTER 10

MY BODY IS THE TEMPLE OF MY SOUL

Energy is needed by everyone to continue with their everyday lives. It's vital when it comes to health and our bodies. It's great for your body to have a lot of energy. There can be life issues that keep us depressed, but as long as you have enough energy, you can get more out of your life and relationships.

Max Travel Club retreats and vacations can be useful if you're feeling not exactly sick, but like you've lost a lot of energy. Energy loss can be a sickness of its own because it can lead to things such as depression. The vacations within the category can help you in restoring that energy so you can get back to doing the things you love.

The vacations not only help with revitalizing your energy, they also get you in touch with your spiritual side. This alone will help you in accomplish tasks such as losing weight, giving up smoking, or changing your diet. It doesn't matter how old you are; the sooner you start, the sooner you'll gain the results you seek. A good tip is to write down your goals and keep checking them so that you can stay motivated.

++

I believe my body is the temple of my soul, and when I treat it that way, it takes care of me as well. You don't need to work at getting healthy; health is something you already have unless you keep disturbing it. When you awaken, you're able to listen to your body and treat it with all the dignity and love your self-respect requires. This is where our retreats will take you—somewhere different in the outside world and in the inside world, which is the most enchanting part and a complete paradigm shift.

Life has got to be about movement. The more you move, the more you feel. The less you move, the less you feel, and the less alive you are. If you're not moving, totally stiff and inflexible, this is known as death. Even if you don't enjoy spending your vacation being physically active, a spa with a medical focus can teach new lifestyle habits and ways of thinking to prevent any potential health problems. If you want a good relationship with anybody, you need to spend some time with them, right? How about spending time with YOU?

"Nothing happens until something moves," Albert Einstein said. It's hard to be depressed when you're absorbed by an effective body program, especially one that turns into a habit after you return home.

Athletes, dancers, and physically active people enjoy life more because they're not doing what inactive, unhealthy, and depressed people are doing. I'm in great shape but I'd still go back on these vacation programs because repetition is the mother of skill. To breathe you have to move, sing, and speak, and if you really want to get closer to your dreams, you have to be at a higher energy level, especially with today's demands. There's just too much to get done, and getting burned out doesn't cut it. Why not enjoy your vacation and gain a fresh perspective while transforming your body, the temple of your soul?

Exercise should be as important to you as a daily meal. This is not to say that vacation should be a painful process; the purpose is actually to get you to enjoy exercise so that you incorporate it into your life.

You're worth it, because nothing is more important than taking care of your body and health daily. If you don't take the time and give this gift to yourself on a regular basis, what makes you think you'll have anything in you to give to others? Nobody wants to be worthless. First you have to value yourself for the universe to value you back.

It's not all just exercise; this *is* a vacation, and many also read and meditate, closing their eyes and letting their minds disappear, and then visualizing what they want for their lives. Some say it's the most powerful and centering thing they've ever done. Normally people realize in one vacation that when you make this a part of your life, you become less stressed and tired during your days. This way you get more out of your days. You're responsible for the days you create, and your days are what make up your life. When you become aware that you're living in a chaotic world, giving this time to yourself first thing in the morning brings you to a peace in which chaos doesn't affect you as it used to. Being calm in a chaotic world is the way to be, and this is the way I know that works.

* * *

Yoga, riflery, canoeing, horseback riding, volleyball, archery, tennis, stretching, swimming, aerobic exercise, wilderness hiking, jogging, walking, whitewater rafting, snorkeling, scuba diving, kayaking—these travel adventures that promote a healthy mental and physical lifestyle can be done while camping, at a resort, or experiencing the lifestyle of a spa.

These trips take place everywhere, though my personal favorites are all around the Caribbean; the six main islands of Hawaii; and Lake Como in Bellagio, Italy, which I consider the most beautiful place in the world. Even if you have physical limitations, these trips offer activities and accommodations for people with a variety of conditions, including hypertension, angina, obesity, arthritis, high cholesterol, diabetes, allergies, and conditions related to stress and aging. Indeed, a vacation for the soul is bound to have a positive impact on nearly any physical condition.

There are very few places on earth that can rival the Dalmatian coast when you want to go sea kayaking. You'll enjoy the sun-soaked coast while you explore the natural terrain on foot as well as by kayak, taking in all the great history and culture, not to mention fabulous cuisine.

* * *

The Buddha said, "To enjoy good health, to bring true happiness to one's family, to bring peace to all, one must first discipline and control one's own mind. If a man can control his mind he can find the way to Enlightenment, and all wisdom and virtue will naturally come to him."

If the world, especially America, made what's learned in these vacations a part of their lives, cancer rates would drop significantly. This is an investment in your longevity. It's fun, it's an electrifying time. Many say, "I want to party when I'm on vacation. I want to celebrate." You *are* celebrating. You're celebrating your body, and nobody said you can't party, because I myself believe in freedom. There's nothing wrong with loving yourself and celebrating every part of your body, like your eyes, which will be seeing the most distinguished and exotic places in the world. Or your ears, which will hear the divine music of the birds in the morning, or waves breaking on the enduring seashore. And don't forget your skin, which allows you to touch and sense things you've never sensed before, like the orange-and-yellow butterfly that landed on my fingertips in the Brazilian rainforest. It reminded me of my preschool in California because of the summer colors.

You will celebrate through illuminating conversations with your new friends at Max Travel Club. You will live in appreciation of every part of your body. The details you never noticed before will come alive in a vacation. This gratefulness for your body becomes addicting, and when you go back home, this new you goes with you. These vacations promote long-term change. Commercial vacations through huge companies do not offer this because it's just not profitable. It's sad to say, but it's true that most people going on commercial vacations aren't aware that they really don't love themselves simply because they don't love their own bodies. The body is connected to the mind and spirit. What's on the inside reflects your standards on the outside. You can't say you love yourself when you abuse yourself physically by drinking too much alcohol, taking drugs, and consuming unhealthy foods. These are all a part of disrespecting yourself. Other people will love you when you love yourself. People come back from vacation burned out and exhausted in need of another vacation. What's the point, when you take your vacation for rest and relaxation, but "letting loose" turns into more stress when you wake with your head spinning and you don't even remember what country you're in? At worst you might come to realize that your passport and your cash are gone. That's exactly why people with higher standards should stick together, yet still have the time of their lives.

Your body offers a constant challenge for improvement and strength, and at the height of its power and passion, you can live life at the highest level.

* * *

My paternal grandfather lived to be 112 in a third-world country without ever seeing a doctor until one year before he died. He didn't know what fast food or Coca-Cola was. He only ate what was grown from the ground, and if he had meat it was in soup so it was soft and tender, which made it easily digestible. Instead of having a Red Bull he had a watermelon a day, which gave him natural sugar, fiber, and water. Grandpa knew that food is nourishment; it's fuel, not something to get feelings from. Exercise is the key to self-love; that's why he walked every day for four hours to and from work. He only took a car or bus two or three times in his life for emergencies. At 112 he was still working full-time out of love for the shoes he created by hand, which lasted a lot longer and were more comfortable than the corporate-branded shoes made by machines in China. At 80 he was still making love every single day when he came home from work; we'd all hear it, and my grandmother confessed. He believed that he never had to worry about his health as long as he was working toward increasing his vitality and strength. He couldn't read or write, but walking four hours a day gave him a great feeling of accomplishment; after his walk, he felt the day was already a success. This gave him even better health, especially with Grandma, because by evening he was on a roll. What Grandpa did with his physical body was a reflection of his entire life. He told my father that if you don't take care of your body with discipline, you don't take care of your life. Grandpa was forty when he married my grandmother, who was then only sixteen. Taking care of himself was vital if he was to live long enough to take care of her. Most of us would do more for others than we would do for ourselves; I'm sure this was his spiritual way of giving. His phenomenal health allowed him to pass the 100 mark, and if it had been all suffering he would not have kept at it. There needs to be a purpose in your life, a reason for you to wake up at 5 a.m., a reason for you to discipline yourself for better health. When your purpose is merely to retire, insurance statistics show you are likely to die after two years. Job dissatisfaction also kills you. You must pursue your passion like

Grandpa, who created every shoe with love even though his hands bled from the work. Do not imagine yourself to be some soulless machine. You have to create a body that moves you and doesn't fatigue quickly.

Exercise embodied into Grandpa's daily hard work made him feel connected to God, or to his creator or source or whatever you want to call it. This is an art that has to be learned; like Eckhart Tolle said, "The power is now." The power is not tomorrow, because tomorrow never comes. Never leave the site of a goal without doing something towards its achievement. I suggest you email (see MaxTravelClub.com for contact information). You have to do something while you're in this state, and the more mighty the action, the more accomplished you become.

It's pleasant to know that the physical vitality you acquire on such a vacation normally awakens your respect for your body, stimulates your insight, elevates your desires, and inspires your personal relationships. Nothing amazing happens through small intentions; inspiration comes from a big goal and taking a big action. That doesn't need to mean hard work; it could be as easy and smart as traveling with me on the next Max Travel Club vacation.

CHAPTER 11

SELF-IMPROVEMENT VACATIONS

"Twenty years from now you will be more disappointed by the things you didn't do than by the ones you did do. So throw off the bowlines. Sail away from the safe harbor. Catch the trade winds in your sails. Explore. Dream. Discover."

—MARK TWAIN

"If you advance confidently in the direction of your own dreams and ever to live the life which you've imagined, you will meet with the success unexpected in common hours."

—HENRY DAVID THOREAU

Self-improvement can be realized in many ways. This is why it isn't surprising that almost every style of vacation you will be introduced to through Max Travel Club can be considered a means to achieve personal development in some way. Even the smallest things, like learning how to knit or losing a few pounds, trigger change in a person, allowing him or her to grow as a human. This chapter will discuss what you will gain from such vacations that can aid in your self-improvement. This means that the club's activities won't start small. Instead of teaching you a small skill, I aim to promote your self-confidence and self-knowledge at the very least. This way you will relate better to others, helping you take a big step more easily.

Taking a vacation for the soul that's focused on self-improvement will help you gain better appreciation and understanding of your psyche. Once you've fully accomplished this, you can be sure to be capable of facing challenges effectively. Goals like independence, self-confidence, self-awareness, and creativity will be attained through vacation activities that involve but are not limited to role-playing, lectures, and art therapy. Nobody but you can give you personal strength, courage, and power. Nobody can get you to believe in your own will, power, and capabilities if you're not willing to do it for yourself. No one but you can give you personal empowerment. So unless you're ready to change your emotions, outlook in life, and perspective on different things, you won't be able to be in the place where you can feel good about yourself and your life.

The only obstacle lying in the way right now is the question, "Where to begin?" Everyone may have an idea what they want to achieve, where they want to be. You may even have that desperation to be happy; the only problem is that the people you deal with and the routines you tend to stick with make things complicated.

If all of these perfectly describe what you're going through, Max Travel Club vacations can help you pull through. They can be the perfect venues for you to learn the skills and gain the mindset needed to reach your potential.

Keep in mind, though, that the programs included won't be able to instantly boost your self-esteem, give you a better capability for understanding things, or make you more creative. There will be a couple of things required on your part, some "work," to put it simply. You can be assured that it won't be much; just enough to help you realize and take pleasure in the best version of you available. It will take some commitment and openness to change, but it will surely be worth it in the end.

Big questions may arise during your travels or retreat: What do I want out of my life at the end? And what do I do every day to get there?

Just remember that you have as much power as anybody else. Every drop of water is equally wet. Wherever you focus, that's where you'll go. That's why the best NBA players visualize scoring before they shoot. You have to think of the end while living in the present, because that's what moves you towards your goals. Yet it's also important to be conscious of the present moment, which is the only thing you have control over. I was always so focused on the future that it gave me anxiety. When I was conscious of the present moment, I felt empowered and in control because I could do something right then. Whether it was an upcoming calculus test or working on my six-pack, NOW was the only time I could work on success. I would visualize success before I went to sleep and when I woke up in the morning. The science behind this is that your brain looks for a way to satisfy your vision because emotions are involved, and it therefore believes the vision is important.

The same creative intelligence that flowed through the blood and hands of Michelangelo as he created David and the *Sistine Chapel* also flows through us. Tapping into it is an art, and it's something I'm in the process of picking up through these sacred vacations, because I'm also a lover of travel and embracing new cultures.

Everything that started in your outside world began in your inside world. This book was something that started in my head and now it's real. You have to create a thing in your head first the way you want it. Through conditioning, most people create in their heads what they *don't* want, and that is what they manifest. But Max Travel Club vacations are the beginning of a brand-new journey on which the best of you shows up every day. When this happens, you'll start appreciating yourself and so will everyone else.

There is so much self-improvement information out there, it's hard to know whom to listen to. Studies have shown that less than 10% of people who buy a self-improvement book read past the first chapter. But on a vacation you have no choice but to become deeply immersed or involved, especially when you're a part of the Max Travel Club. Any individual who takes one of these self-improvement vacations is one of the few who *do*, compared to the majority, who merely talk.

Successful people aren't lucky. There are people out there who have only 2% of my wisdom and knowledge but are still ridiculously successful. Why? They do what they know and they take major action, and if it goes wrong they go a different route until they get what their heart desires. Those same successful people aren't perfect; even if, say, their finances are perfect, their relationships probably aren't, and therefore they could benefit from one of our relationship vacations. Max Travel Club is for quality people who want more out of life. And those of you trying to raise your standards should put yourselves in an environment that can take you higher.

There are certain things happy people do on a regular basis that make them happy. You can keep reading about it or you can do it on vacation, where it stays in your system when you come back. This vacation is for unreasonable people, because reasonable people live average lives. Reasonable people wake up in the morning and don't know why they're alive or what they want their day to be about. Reasonable people spend almost half their day on Facebook (the new coffee shop), talking mostly nonsense. The more you demand from yourself—the more you're willing to be "unreasonable" —the more you'll get out of these self-improvement vacations. You will create an extraordinary psychology that will manifest a phenomenal life.

When the president and CEO of Trodat, a $200 million company, came to visit me from Austria for a meeting in downtown L.A., I asked him, "How'd you do it? How did you get to where you are?" He said, "I don't focus on what I have to do, I focus on what I want." If you're scared of a self-improvement vacation, maybe it's because you associate discipline with a lack of freedom instead of with freedom itself. Discipline has power, just like the Trodat CEO said: "I decide and I do." That's discipline, and that has power. Most people keep thinking that they'll be happy once they complete a goal, but unfortunately, that is so not true. The CEO also told me you can't make money working for somebody else unless you're an investor. This country rewards those who know how to sell and market. Having a job and running your own business on the side means no time for TV or cleaning up your house because you have to focus on selling to get out of your job. Sell anything that's a solution to a problem, or that you're passionate about and love.

Most people think they'll be happy once they complete a goal, but unfortunately, that is so not true. Making lots of money on a sale only made me happy for so long. I actually felt really empty after I got an A + on my finance exam. I had ignored many moments of my life for weeks by immersing myself in studying, and I made nothing else matter but my exam. My purpose and yours is available at every moment of our lives, but I didn't know what my purpose was at the time. I was in my little box studying instead of taking a few moments and putting myself in situations where I didn't know what things meant or what to do. Yet it's in those environments where we grow the most.

Being stuck in my comfort zone studying didn't allow me to grow, and we're only happy when we grow and expand no matter what our age. When you stop growing you might as well be dead, because you're sure going to feel dead and empty on the inside. If you don't keep stepping into the unknown or if you don't have faith you instantly die internally. You'll suffer an emotional death. You have to trust or you'll be stuck in your box and rotting away. You have to have faith in yourself to live, to start a business, to enter a relationship. When you lose your life emotionally and you're discontent, physical death is right around the corner.

Researchers prove the mind–body connection is a physical reality. Something that doesn't expand your life emotionally or physically is something you don't need. Studies on heart patients reveal that those who felt isolated from their family, community, and especially their spirituality were more susceptible to disease. The focus on how long we're going to live doesn't allow us to live a quality life. We need to focus on how we're going to live while we're here. How can you win the game of life if you don't know what your purpose is? You can't, and you will always feel like you're losing. Don't have too many rules in life about how you should be; this will make you completely miserable like certain friends and family of mine who curse everybody on the road. Focus instead on your purpose and try to take joy in something as simple as a smile. When you live your life in reaction to the world, you remain a very unhappy person. Try to be an observer, because it's not your job to change someone or the world.

What is the purpose of your life? You decide. Keep writing until you have something you like. The environment Max Travel Club vacations provide will help you realize your purpose, but for now, if you're writing, don't be a gangster or extremist—make sure you don't have to die to achieve your purpose. And remember that sometimes not getting your dream gives you what you're really destined for. It's like in the movie *Field of Dreams*: if you build it, they will come.

* * *

You have to hire a housekeeper so you can just focus on running a business. As your business sales pick up, then hire a professional scheduler; there is no time to waste, so you need to be professional about the most valuable thing given to you on this earth, and that's your time. When things really start picking up, you need a bookkeeper because all your focus should be just on sales and marketing through building.

My mother was raised to feel guilty if she ate more than anybody else while visiting someone's house. She raised me the same. Once we were visiting my uncle, and I felt hungry. I weighed only eighty pounds, but my mother made me feel guilty for eating that extra food. But when I looked at the hungry raccoon going through the trash that night, I saw that it didn't care or feel guilty about eating. If a raccoon is hungry, it respects its own needs and fulfills them. A raccoon is a go-getter for its own needs.

Remember: You have as much power as anybody else. Every drop of water is equally wet. Everything in life has a purpose.

WEALTH

Many think the mind, body, and spirit have nothing to do with being wealthy. But that's completely wrong, because the only way to be wealthy is to add more value to other people's lives than anybody else does. IT'S THE ONLY WAY. If there's a misalignment or an imbalance among your mind, body, and spirit, how can you add more value to other people's lives? Your income is in direct proportion to your contribution! You can't contribute to your full potential if you have personal needs that aren't being met, or if you have inner conflicts. You can't give to others what you haven't given to yourself first. You can't contribute when you haven't taken care of your own mind, body, and spirit first. I can't stress this enough: contributing to society and the world starts first within yourself, with your mind, body, and spirit.

Wealth starts with your mind. As human beings we sometimes get what we *have* to have, not what we *should* have. We have to make it a must to be abundant and wealthy and to have more than enough. The best advice wealthy advisers have given me is to write a paragraph on why I have to be wealthy. Once your mind, body, and spirit are balanced, it's a lot easier to see your life like a business in which you don't feel guilty if you have a profit at the end of the year. My father told me a magic formula: spend less than you earn, and invest the difference while in a balanced state. You're not really wealthy until you're abundant in all areas, including your mind, body, and spirit.

The purpose of a goal is the person we become in the process of achieving it. Expand financially by expanding spiritually first. Take your thoughts, ideas, and desires and convert them to your physical reality. When you're in alignment with your inner purpose first, wealth is much easier to obtain. There are many people who have everything but are unhappy; therefore we must be happy and at peace first. The right vacation will start you off on the right path.

More conscious people with money would be a great gift to this planet. There's nothing beautiful about poverty, or Mommy and Daddy not being able to feed the kids even though both parents are working. It's ugly when money stops circulating. If you lose money, a lot of other people will also lose the money they need to make a living. The more you have, the more others make because you have it. Making money out of your innocence is more than possible.

Seize opportunities when they come your way. Think of the acronym POOR: Passing Over Opportunity Repeatedly. But don't regret opportunities you've lost in the past. As Eckhart Tolle said, the power is now, so stay aware of the opportunity that comes in your life from now on. The self-actualized way to wealth is being detached from the outcome of profit, and being focused on serving to quadruple your income.

Walt Disney was told by every loan institution that his idea was absolutely ridiculous, that no one would go for it. He was turned down by more than three hundred bankers until he finally found someone to fund his vision. Imagine the loss to thousands of children and families if Disney had allowed these bankers to limit his idea. People who put down your ideas may mean well—they don't want you to get your hopes up and get hurt. But we must understand that those people's reality is based on the information that's given to them. I believe people do the best they can with the resources they have. Successful people pursue quality information that will nourish their lives. They learn to trust their instincts.

CHAPTER 12

THOUSANDS NOW ENHANCE THEIR RELATIONSHIPS WHO NEVER THOUGHT THEY COULD

"And ever has it been that love knows not its own depth until the hour of separation."

—KHALIL GIBRAN

"When you meet with people at work or whenever it maybe, give them your fullest attention. You are no longer there primarily as a person but as a field of awareness, of alert presence. The arising of that unifying field of awareness between human beings is the most essential factor in relationships on the new earth."

—ECKHART TOLLE

We all interact with many people on a daily basis, but we tend to get caught up in our busy lives. Sometimes we forget what is really important. When we let busyness take over, it tends to interfere and even mess up some of our close relationships. If you know you're not having much fun in your life, it's time to stop and think about ways to balance your personal lives with business and other social events. Taking a nice vacation away can help restore the balance you need. It's great for making us go deep within and trying to prioritize things without the interference of stress or other people.

If you are in a troubled relationship, you must start thinking about what's wrong and how to go about changing it to make it better. As soon as you figure that out, it's best to stick to the plan and execute it. Every three months, even stable couples need to get away for a few days to remain healthy. They must get out of their usual surroundings. This is also true for family members and friends, because when you spend time with someone day after day doing something that's fun, it bonds you for life. There is absolutely no replacement for time if you want to keep friendships and relationships for a lifetime. This must be an individual decision, though, because if you feel your beloved needs space, consider going on separate vacations. Not every vacation that benefits your relationship has to be with your partner. A spiritual experience that strengthens you can bring new strength to your relationship. The point is "to electrify the spiritual impulse that animates all of life," as Wuthnow said. And Stephanie Ocko explained, "When you fall in love, the erotic pulls open doors to new worlds and draws you to new galaxies; your love is everywhere at once. Spiritual attraction rides the same path. In your heightened state, you begin to see God in others. And there's no turning back."

If you decide not to go as a couple on the same vacation, you'll have an opportunity to look at the relationship issues in your life. Most people avoid facing a conflicted relationship until they reach a crisis point.

Are your relationships worth taking the time to enhance? If so, these will be great vacations for you.

If you do decide to take your partner, remind them as specifically as possible of the positive times you've shared. This might also give you the opportunity to review your life together. Try to get your partner to list some positive times as well, and remind yourself of these while you're on such a vacation. At the end of that same day or vacation, repeat back to your partner the words they used that most moved you.

* * *

A vacation for the soul in Iceland, Sweden, or Norway would include experiencing the northern lights in all of their glory. Sharing this experience goes beyond taking a date to the movies; such a magical experience is cherished for life and can create a very strong bond between two people.

If Scandinavia is too cold for you, then enjoy the ultimate honeymoon experience in the exotic Maldives. Spend days and nights at the beautiful beaches, dine outdoors under the stars with your loved one, and dare to experience a romantic getaway at a secluded island nearby. Indulge in relaxing and rejuvenating spa treatments and massages, or laze around in the sun. This is the perfect place for honeymoons, and you will definitely want to come back to relive the experience.

Adventurous couples would also enjoy diving in the warm waters of Maldives, where the sea is clear enough to see beautiful coral reefs and other marine creatures. Dive in and see the interesting marine life up close. There are diving instructors available for hire if you are beginners.

Maldives is also rich in culture. Open your eyes, heart, and mind to experience the rich, exotic cultural heritage of the people of Maldives.

Enjoy Maldivian music, art, and crafts for an experience that money can never buy.

If you choose to go to northern Europe, you can spend two nights in Prague, taking in the spectacular architecture, and then cruise between Germany and Budapest, enjoying the Christmas celebrations onboard and on land. Take time off in Venice to watch the gondolas, or stroll through the streets of Rome. Cruising, touring, and traveling throughout Europe on a vacation for the soul is an ideal way for you to see the main European high spots and the beauty of the rivers.

Some couples who are looking for an experience similar to both Maldives and northern Europe choose to go to Greece and Turkey, or Czechoslovakia, Germany, and Hungary. Summer is a great time to travel to Italy, and in Greece and Turkey you can enjoy the sunshine and the historic sites, like Rome and Ephesus. Take a trip to northern Italy in the winter and enjoy the traditional Christmas street markets with their food stalls and twinkling lights.

* * *

A committed relationship is by far the most important alliance anyone ever experiences in life. If the spiritual forces are allied for a definitive purpose, they yield the greatest of all powers for success financially, physically, mentally, emotionally, and spiritually. The spiritual needs to come first, of course, because anything I or anybody else creates starts first in the mind, as a vision. Creating an extraordinary relationship also starts in the mind. This is because we are spiritual beings having a human experience.

We have to keep reminding ourselves that a relationship is about *relating*, whether it's to your spouse, significant other, best friend, family, even customers and business associates. Everything in your life that doesn't grow dies; this is true of everything in the universe. If your relationships with others, with your your body, and with your mind don't grow, they begin to die as well. When you're green, you grow; if you think you've completely matured, you rot.

I have so many things going, I sometimes wish I could just have someone else handle my relationships. But that would rob me of the chance to grow and expand by natural development so I can get what I deserve in my life. To achieve success, I tried to make a sacrifice by cutting everybody off and just focusing on myself, but I didn't have the deepest level of love to share with the supreme being, family, friends, or especially my significant other.

Another law of life is that YOU must contribute to your relationships. If you don't, you will be eliminated not only from your relationships but from the universe. For example, an older family member whom I loved very much, God rest his soul, had a major opium addiction that took priority even over his family, wife, and kids. Instead of investing in the future of his children, he left them and invested in the drug. God forgive him for being as unconscious as he was. When he started aging he realized he was all alone. Everybody around him had either died early or left and love was missing from his life, so he'd smoke away the pain. This is not a place you want to be. You need to raise your standards when it comes to improving your relationships.

Falling in love and beginning an intimate relationship helped form my soul, spirit, and emotion and allowed me to enjoy life to the fullest. I never took any drugs, yet I saw everything differently, as if it had more color or was a fourth dimension, an awakening. Handling this relationship poorly and being unconscious of what I was doing led to pain and sorrow. If we're healthy, we naturally want to keep growing and expanding. Other than enjoying your travel on these relationship-enhancement vacations, you will also be made aware of where the gaps are in your relationship. Where are you now? You're either in an intimate relationship or you're not. Most people want to be in one but are too scared and associate way too much pain with romantic relationships, so they convince themselves that they don't need it. But how can you have joy without sometimes having pain? How can you know darkness without light? On this type of vacation, you will learn how to get value from the darkness.

* * *

Before I get into more depth and meaning, the South Pacific and Bora Bora in particular are phenomenal getaway locales and have been for decades. There are soft white beaches and clear azure and teal seas that allow you to see the bottom of the ocean floor, even in deep water. A sun-draped island, gentle subtropical winds, and warm weather all conspire to make Bora Bora a sun-worshipper's paradise. Bora Bora is also home to some of the most well-known resorts you will ever find in a tropical setting.

If you need a break from an overly conscious, aware, and meaningful day, Bora Bora has an amazing nightlife as well, with award-winning nightclubs at any of the island's resorts. If you are looking to recharge your internal batteries during your stay in Bora Bora, you can enjoy any one of a number of resort-style spas located on the island. The resorts also offer personalized and discreet in-house massage services for couples.

A railway vacation is also one you will be talking about for years to come. The Canadian Rockies are a protected area with world-class ski resorts. A railway vacation is a great way of experiencing the breathtaking views of Canada while soul-searching and trying to relate to your partner.

* * *

It is for people who want more from their relationships, or who want to get out of them and start fresh.

The saddest thing is responding to your partner as if he or she is someone else, as if you're talking to your relatives or friends. What's more depressing is talking about your partner as if he or she is a horrible person when you're just too scared to leave. My personal rule #1 is to NEVER EVER talk bad about your partner to others because it only makes you look ridiculous. Why are you with the person, then? Don't even talk bad about him or her when it's over, because it's over! Instead of expanding on what you don't want or like, it's time to just focus on what you want and to stop wasting any time.

When it comes to your past, my best friend, Gabe Kahsay, would say, "It is what it is." He would tell me to move on from there. All the stress in my life has come from making things bigger than they really are, and I'm sure it's like that for you too. I've really injured people in all types of relationships by assuming the worst, especially in my intimate relationship. This caused a lot of suffering for myself and my significant other at the time because when you injure someone you care about, you're only hurting yourself because you're sharing it. You're attacking your teammates and your partner when you should be playing together.

To have a life you have to have some movement, so if you feel you're in a rut and your relationship isn't going anywhere, there are vacations that can shift or enhance your connection. If you could have your relationship any way you want it, this is the place where you can create it. We're so busy with the small things in our lives that we take no time for what's important. The quality of your life shows in the quality of your relationships. That drunk person you met at the club in Cancun probably doesn't remember you.

A lot of my business buddies aren't happy in their relationships because they're only sharing their ideas, when they need to be sharing their emotions and feelings as well. This goes for both parties. Relationship vacations involve feeling, hearing, and experiencing the soul. There is so much power in unity. Traveling with Max Travel Club brings a certain amount of relatedness that comes from physical proximity to other people. Just as your personal relationship is a place you go to give instead of get, this is the same type of psychology you should bring on vacation.

Do you have a relationship, or do you have a business transaction? All my friends in the Hollywood scene and my entrepreneur friends in general are always looking at what they can get out of their so-called relationships. They are driven mad by their egos. They are looking to gain with every action, but if you want a loyal customer, wife, girlfriend, or friend, you have to be focused on giving without expecting anything back. If you treat people right and they genuinely like you, they will come back to you regardless of a little higher price or another better-looking guy or girl. A relationship is about unlimited giving. If you spend the most on your customer or give the most to your partner, you've created a real relationship.

My own intimate relationship began to die when I set up all these rules, like "this means that" or "you can't do this," with no *love* being involved. The more rules you have in your life and in your relationships, the more you will suffer. If a baby doesn't receive love it dies, and fear of not being loved is a primary human fear. Adults are just big babies anyway. Sharing and connection are what bring joy in life. The sad thing is that all my buddies who laugh at my advice because they're macho and say they only care about the money feel an emptiness inside, or are not aware of their emptiness because they're living in chaos.

I congratulate my determined friends, but some of them are mainly determined because they feel if they achieve a lot or succeed, they'll eventually be loved, which takes away from the whole relationship building process. Many of them fail to recognize that the basis of a good relationship starts with loving themselves, and if they're going to a relationship to get love because they're rich, they've forgotten the meaning behind a relationship in the first place. They are basically saying they only deserve love because of their material possessions, which is sad because I'm sure they're worth more than that.

There are people who love each other even when they lose everything. These types of life events can even bring people closer, enabling them to see the light in each other's eyes. If you wanted somebody to feel totally loved by you, what would you do? Would you show them your car, or tell them of your accomplishments? This is what people do when they aren't aware and connected to what they love about themselves. I learned this from Louise L. Hay.

My ex got tired of my saying "I love you" without looking into her eyes. She said they were just words. I eventually realized it's because I couldn't look into my own eyes in the mirror and say, "I love you." I didn't love myself at the time and I wondered why I wasn't getting respect from my close family. They felt like I was a taker, not a giver. I couldn't give to someone else what I haven't given to myself.

Psychological studies show that people who received a lot of love in childhood are more confident and aren't desperate for love when they get older, and as a result they actually receive more love from the universe because they don't see love lacking in their lives. The children who didn't receive love are always looking for it and see it as something that's lacking in their lives. Once these children grow up and learn to truly love themselves for who they are, they start attracting that love into their life because they become givers, not creating a deficient universe for themselves anymore.

A relationship-focused vacation is one where you'll learn to appreciate and recognize your existence as a great human being, and gaining great appreciation for and love of yourself. Even if you already love yourself, this will take you to another level. There is only so much I can put in a book. What I describe here is only 2% of the whole experience.

I was listening to the radio one day and heard Usher sing about how nobody had given him anything when he was broke, but as soon as he became famous, everybody gave him stuff for free. The same thing goes with loving yourself. When you're poor on the inside and don't believe you're worth it, that's exactly how you'll be treated. When you love yourself, the universe will give you much more love than you really need. It's a law of nature!

My friends who have jumped from relationship to relationship tend to stereotype all men and women as being the same, and then wonder why they attract the same kind of person every time. They are completely unconscious that it's because they're taking themselves with them as they jump into new relationships every two months or two days.

If you bring your partner to one of these relationship vacations, it will prove to be a magical breakthrough. You will learn how you can complement each other despite your differences, and satisfy each other's needs in every way possible. If you're single, you will realize the importance of being clear about what you want, not just what you'll settle for. It takes time and awareness to look inside to see what it is you really want without distractions.

A vacation will transform your motive and perspective. Instead of getting what happens to show up in your life, like 99% of society, you'll be totally focused and clear about what you're looking for, which will make it so much easier to attract what you really want, seeing through all the clutter because of the awareness you've gained. Remember, here you get clear about what you want, and that's what the focus is. My unhappy friends with whom I don't associate anymore are still focused on what they don't want and still complain that that's what keeps showing up into their lives.

On this relationship vacation you realize who you have to be and what you have to do to have a higher quality of life and to attract that same type of person if you're already not with him or her. When you apply intrinsic excellence towards your life, family, and relationships, you can pretty much attract anybody you want.

If you're with your partner, you learn how to deliver and satisfy their needs. And it's time you'll get to spend with each other to see what you both really want and don't want in a relationship. The reason this is best done on a vacation is because in your regular lives, one or both of you might not have felt safe sharing their needs. You both need to break out of your shells.

If your relationship is already great, you can still take it to another level by the end of your next vacation. On the other hand, if you're in a relationship only because you fear economic distress or what people might think of you because you feel like a failure, you'll really need an awakening, and these vacations are more than necessary. You deserve to share a profound life with someone at a heartfelt level.

Since your relationships are where the juice in your life is, this is more important than any other area of your life. It can directly affect all areas of your life in a positive or negative manner. When my father had major problems with my mother, his sales in business fell. When I had problems with my father, my university work really suffered, and it took me much longer than necessary to get out of school. It also made me burn out to where I just didn't have it in me to work out or to concentrate on eating right.

I've realized through observing family members and others that they're so focused on the institution of marriage, they forget that happiness and living a good life created by the marriage is the most important part. I've also seen travel to exotic destinations create stimulating conversation every night, talking till 3 a.m. before and after the vacation.

Being attracted only lasts so long, and attraction eventually leads to boredom. I've seen many people cheat on each other when they've lost their sense of connection. I've heard many judgmental people say, "How's this person with that person? How does this other person even turn them on?" They're missing the point. Maybe this attractive person they think has bad taste has had many opportunities to choose better-looking people, but the connection she's established with this other person keeps them together. Please stop criticizing couples and saying you feel sorry for them because of who they have to be when it's that connection that keeps them together for a hundred years. That's the kind of connection that, when lost, makes one person pass away right after their spouse does.

If you're already with someone, a good exercise before you come on this vacation is to write or share moments you've enjoyed with them. Also, I don't agree with everything in the movie *The Secret*, but writing down what you enjoy about the person definitely does shift your mind to focus on the positive, which is a great place to be before taking a vacation together. If you don't sharpen your focus on the little details you enjoy about each other, the challenges will ambush all the good.

What destroys most great relationships is that the hearts connect but the personalities are out to kill one another. Two people loving each other is not enough because you have to be conscious; living on this Earth, the less conscious you are, the more disassociated you are from the truth about yourself. You come with love *into* a situation, but you don't lead with love. Most likely it's because of your ego that you're not expressing the beingness of your love. Instead you express your fear, which is ignited by your ego, and you can be ridiculous enough to assume that the person can and should read your mind. The love of my life said, "It's not enough for you to tell me you love me, I have to feel your love." And it's up to you to figure out how your partner/lover/significant other needs to feel love. Different people need to have love expressed in different ways.

Ladislaus Boros knew a great secret: "Everything true and great grows in silence." Wouldn't all the decisions in our lives, especially in our relationships, benefit from less distraction and more stillness? Vacations for the soul are a big part of my spiritual discipline, and I would absolutely love to share that experience with you because love and connection are human needs.

Free Super Luxury Travel Postcard book Plus Free Surprise Gifts
Triggered to Your Personality by
e-mailing max@maxtravelclub.com
e-mail me your
-name
-address
For Optional Surprise Free Gift <u>add</u> your
-occupation
-hobbies

www.ingramcontent.com/pod-product-compliance
Lightning Source LLC
Chambersburg PA
CBHW042337150426
43195CB00001B/27